MORE

ISBN 10: 1-936196-00-X
ISBN 13: 978-1936196-00-5
LCCN: 2009942944

C&R Press
812 Westwood Ave.
Chattanooga, TN 37405

www.crpress.org

MORE

Barbara Crooker

Table of Contents

1.

2.

3.

one

"Everybody's got a hungry heart."
—*Bruce Springsteen*

How the Trees on Summer Nights Turn into a Dark River,

how you can never reach it, no matter how hard you try,
walking as fast as you can, but getting nowhere,
arms and legs pumping, sweat drizzling in rivulets;
each year, a little slower, more creaks and aches, less breath.
Ah, but these soft nights, air like a warm bath, the dusky wings
of bats careening crazily overhead, and you'd think the road
goes on forever. Apollinaire wrote, "What isn't given to love
is so much wasted," and I wonder what I haven't given yet.
A thin comma moon rises orange, a skinny slice of melon,
so delicious I could drown in its sweetness. Or eat the whole
thing, down to the rind. Always, this hunger for more.

The Sun Lays Down its Light

This cardinal's a scolding French *maman*, going *vite, vite, vite,*
telling us that time is running away, slipping quickly,
like the sunlight-laced water in this stream,
laughing as it runs over rocks, twists
around the gravel bend, where the chartreuse fans
of skunk cabbage lazily sway. There's a catbird
in a charcoal business suit who's just stepped outside
for lunch break to take the air, thick with birdsong
and longing. The sun is laying down its light like a jazz
saxophone lays out its brassy line, threads
in and out of the melody, notes spreading thick
as honey. My old friend and my mother begin
their last days; neither will see another spring.
I don't know how to say goodbye. Time should be
more elastic, we should be able to pull it
like molasses taffy, stretch out its tawny sweetness.
Vite, vite, vite, the cardinal sings again.

Geology

Place a stone in the palm of your hand;
it lies there, inert, nothing but itself.
It revels in its stoniness, its solidity.
It gathers light, rises from the plains,
a mountain in miniature, notches and ridges
carved by weather, strata and stria,
the pressure of time, the rough places,
planed. A climber might try for the pinnacle,
looking for toe holds in cracks and crevasses.
The way up is never easy. The air thins.
From the peak, the horizon falls away.
Borders are meaningless. The stone rests
in your hand. It sings its one long song.
Something about eternity.
Something about the sea.

Sanctus

A goldfinch, bright as a grace note, has landed
on a branch across the creek that mutters
and murmurs to itself as it rushes on, always
in a hurry. The *ee oh lay* of a wood thrush echoes
from deep in the forest, someplace green. In paintings,
the Holy Ghost usually takes the form of a stylized
dove, its whiteness a blaze of purity. But what if
it's really a mourning dove, ordinary as daylight
in its old coat, nothing you'd ever notice.
When he rises from the creek and the light flares
behind, his tail is edged in white scallops,
shining. And when he opens his beak,
isn't he calling your name,
sweet and low, *You, you, you?*

Finches, Little Pats of Butter on the Wing,

hang upside down at the thistle feeder
full of shiny black seeds, not from those spiny-
thorned purple tufts we see in fields, but from
Nyger plants, recently respelled to avoid
racial slurs. O praise political correctness!
Once in a while, they get it right.

And now, everything bursts into bloom,
the great bouquets of trees, our largest
perennials: double ruffled cherries, purple-
leafed plum, flowering pear. It's May, when
everything you planted flourishes, nothing leggy,
overgrown, or gone to seed. Once in a while,
you get it right. The lawn flows, a river
of green silk. How did all this loveliness
spring from the dark?

White

Everyone has this dream one time or another:
it's that math class you signed up for but forgot
to attend and now it's the final, white test pages
spread out before you, but you haven't the foggiest
where to begin. The formulas are unsolvable,
unreachable as the chalky clouds smearing
the horizon above the vast blackboard of the sea.
It's so quiet you can hear each minute tick by,
as frantically you search your memory
for the answer that isn't there. Or there's that other
dream, the one where you remembered your books,
homework, the essay you wrote late last night,
you just forgot to get dressed, and there you are,
naked, your white body a plucked chicken
on a platter, everyone's laughing, and there's
nothing you can hide behind, no way to cover
the cellulite, the lumps, the bulges. Which are
like these clouds, fat and puffy, that slowly traverse
the sky. They don't care who passes this test,
don't measure their bodies against each other's.
They swell with water vapor, diminish with wind,
bleach white with dazzle and sunsplash. White,
the memory of itself, what you see before
you fall into bed at night, into the arms of sleep,
or the long tunnel you swim through
on that last journey home.

Salt

It pours from the dark blue sky
of a cardboard cylinder
where a little girl
stands with an open umbrella,
etched in white.
Without it, bread would not rise.
Ham would not cure. Soup
would lose it savor. Language
its fizz. Swimmers would sink
under heavy waves. Morning's
eggs, dull on the plate. It speaks
in tongues, to wake ours up. Even
when spilled on the table,
the tiny crystals spell
their secret names, dots
to be connected, a puzzle
to be solved, the private code
that only you
could transcribe.

What You Want

is more than refrigerator art,
more than making sack lunches.
You want a bad boy for a lover,
one who'd make a lousy husband,
a wanderer on a Harley. What you want
has high cholesterol, lots of sodium,
and no fiber, nothing seven-grain-sprouted,
hearth-baked, with added-oat-bran.
Bring on the heavy cream.
What you want comes in five flavors,
and all of them are chocolate:
milk, mocha, alpine white, semi-, bittersweet.
What you want never goes on sale,
or, if it does, by appointment only,
fifth Tuesday, dark of the moon, Scorpio
rising. Is never found at garage sales.
What you want
would feel so good on your skin
you'd never wear clothes again.
What you want is not found
at K-Mart, naked in the blue light.
What you want isn't canned by Campbell's
or baked by elves; it must be flown in
from Rome or brought from Alaska
by dog sled. What you want isn't played
on AM radio, borrowed from public libraries.
Isn't found in Webster's or Roget's.
Never gives double coupons, green stamps,
rebates or money-back guarantees;
gains no interest, gathers no moss.

Ode to Chocolate

I hate milk chocolate, don't want clouds
of cream diluting the dark night sky,
don't want pralines or raisins, rubble
in this smooth plateau. I like my coffee
black, my beer from Germany, wine
from Burgundy, the darker, the better.
I like my heroes complicated and brooding,
James Dean in oiled leather, leaning
on a motorcycle. You know the color.

Oh, chocolate! From the spice bazaars
of Africa, hulled in mills, beaten,
pressed in bars. The cold slab of a cave's
interior, when all the stars
have gone to sleep.

Chocolate strolls up to the microphone
and plays jazz at midnight, the low slow
notes of a bass clarinet. Chocolate saunters
down the runway, slouches in quaint
boutiques; its style is *je ne sais quoi*.
Chocolate stays up late and gambles,
likes roulette. Always bets
on the *noir*.

Ode to Olive Oil

From hard green drupes
of bitter flesh, a river
of gold and green— From
trees bent like old women
whose leaves flash
olive drab to silver
in the hot breeze,
a bowlful of summer—

The transmutation:
flesh of the tree to liquid amber—
Picked by hand, collected in nets,
the willow baskets fill with fruit,
spill into wooden boxes,
are crushed between wheels
of stone, pits and all.

You can marry it with *aceto balsamico*
to dress your salad, gilding emerald
and ruby leaves— You can ladle
it on white beans and sage, drizzle
it on sun-warm tomatoes, lace it
in minestrone, bathe garlic heads
for roasting. You can make it
into soap, rub it with mint leaves
for migraine. Take a spoonful
to prevent hangover. Mash
it with rosemary and all the pain
is gone from creaky knees.

Velvet on the tongue. The light
of late afternoons. I am eating
sunshine, spread on bread;
primroses open in my mouth.
My chin gleams yellow,
the opposite of a halo,
but one surely even the saints
would recognize and bless.

Demeter

It was November when my middle daughter
descended to the underworld. She fell
off her horse straight into Coma's arms.
He dragged her down, wrapped her in a sleep
so deep I thought I would never see her again.
Each day, the light grew dimmer, as Earth
moved away from sun. I was not writing this story;
no one knew the ending, not even the neurosurgeons
with their fancy machines. Every twenty-four
hours, she slipped further away. I called
and called her name, offered to trade places,
ate six pomegranate seeds, their bleeding garnets
tart on the tongue. Her classmates took
their SATs, wrote their entrance essays. She
went down into the darkness, another level
deeper. I was ready to deliver her to college,
watch her disappear into a red brick dorm, green
trees waving their arms in welcome. Not this,
season without ending, where switches changed
the darkness to light, and breath was forced
through tubes and machines, their steady hum
the only music of the dim room. The shadows
under her eyes turned blue-violet, and pneumonia
filled her lungs.

And then, one morning, slight as the shift
from winter to spring, her eyelids fluttered,
and up she swam, a slippery rebirth,
and the light that came into the room
was from a different world.

Snapshot

They were drinking coffee and smiling.
You saw the photograph.
There was a small table, a pot
of geraniums. Two dark cups,
simmering. You don't see the accident,
the daughter in a coma.
The weeks the parents didn't speak.
The way she turned from him in the dark.
You don't see the daughter's return,
the slurred speech, the stumbling gait.
The way she had to learn everything over
again, ABCs to cursive, kindergarten
to physics. She lost her balance,
couldn't dance, but the teacher let her
use the *barre* in the studio. Small steps
led back to *pointe*. Later, a May
recital, the mother sobbing
in the auditorium. The camera
didn't catch this. The camera
is a liar. It edits every frame,
shows only the sunlight
falling through the plane trees.
It doesn't know how to count:
minutes, hours, long black
nights. That December,
it would have showed
a happy family on a glossy
card. It's a blind
eye, doesn't show
what's missing.
The girl went off to college.

The parents took back
their lives. But nothing
was ever the same. The ground
had shifted. They knew
that loss was waiting, only
around the corner. They are
drinking coffee, and smiling.

Narrative

This morning's miracle: dawn turned up its dimmer,
set the net of dew on the lawn to shining. The sky,
lightly iced with clouds, stretched from horizon
to horizon, not an inch to spare, and later, the sun
splashed its bucket of light on the ground. But it's
never enough. The hungry heart wants more: another
ten years with the man you love, even though you've had
thirty; one more night rinsed in moonlight, bodies twisted
in sheets, one more afternoon under the plane trees
by the fountain, with a jug of red wine and bits of bread
scattered around. More, even though the grasses
are glowing in the dying light, and the hills are turning
all the syllables of lavender, as evening draws the curtains,
turns on the lamps. One more book, one more story,
as if all the words weren't already written, as if all the plots
haven't been used, as if we didn't know the ending already,
as if this time, we thought it could turn out differently.

two

"There is no remedy to love but to love more."
—Henry David Thoreau

Surfer Girl

I'm walking on the beach this cold brisk morning,
the bleached sea grass bending in the wind, when there,
up ahead, in the pewter waves, I see a surfer in his wet suit,
sleek as a seal, cutting in and out of the curl, shining in the light.
I'm on the far side of sixty, athletic as a sofa, but this is where
the longing starts, the yearning for another life, the one
where I'm lithe and long-limbed, tanned California bronze,
short tousled hair full of sunshine. The life where I shoulder my board,
stride into the waves, dive under the breakers, and rise; my head shaking
off water like a golden retriever. I am waiting for that perfect wave
so I can crouch up and catch it, my arms out like wings, slicing back
and forth in the froth, wind at my back, sea's slick metal polished
before me. Nothing more important now than this balance between
water and air, the rhythm of in and out, staying ahead of the break,
choosing my line like I choose these words, writing my name
on water, writing my name on air.

Our Lady of Rocamadour

We have climbed these two hundred steps,
not on our knees as medieval penitents,
but on our modern feet, yours with the high
and aching arches, mine with their bunions
and hammer toes, a cobbler's nightmare,
trudging up the stairs and cobblestoned
paths. In the twelfth century chapel, she waits,

the Black Madonna, where she has brooded
over centuries of pilgrims, cockle
shells pinned to their breasts,
the coracles of their hopes
setting sail. She is serene, shining
in her ebony wood, a dark star.
She holds her small son, reigns
over the history of loss.

I pray for my damaged son, rocking
as if tossed on stormy seas and chanting,
"Goats, goats, goats. They always
make me laugh." What can we do
with so much tenderness?

Keep walking, one foot
in front of the other, on this stony
road. Blink in the sun
that nearly blinds us
as we stumble out of the chapel.
Below the parapets, hawks soar on thermals,
their bright wings keeping them aloft
on waves of air, imperceptible
as gravity or light.

Excuses, Excuses

Excuse me. I didn't mean to eat
that last piece of cheesecake
when it called my name
at three am. Can you excuse
me for not being interested in how
a car actually works, those pistons
and rings, or why the stock market
rises and falls? I think I can excuse
just about anything, even the past,
my other life, where my first husband
stayed out all night, after the bars
had closed. I swallowed
his excuses with my morning
coffee; let the oily bitterness
still my tongue. I can excuse
my compulsive son's obsessions,
as he tells us once more the year
that Elvis died, picking at the scab
on his head until it bleeds, because
I know he has no choice. The sweetness
of the creamy cake slides off my fork
like eating a cloud. The engine
of our new marriage hums and purrs.
I would choose you again if I met
you at a party, even if I could see
the future, the damaged child,
the bodies that creak and sag.
No excuses. A cup of moonlight
is pouring in the window;
it glints and winks off your silver hair.

Peaches

In pecks and bushels
at Shoemaker's stand, they fill
the baskets with their heft,
their plush shoulders, handfuls
of light. Cut in wedges arranged
on a blue-glazed plate:
slices of sun in the August sky.
Take and eat, for this is the essence
of summer, given for you, in spite of
winter's sure return, the short gray days,
the icy nights. Right now, there are wheat
fields and sweet corn, daylilies and chicory
by the dusty roadsides; in the long dusk,
fireflies decorate the grass, rise up
to meet their doubles, the stars.

Tonight, there's fried chicken and sliced
tomatoes, hot biscuits, butter,
and peach jam. And later, you,
next to me on the rumpled
sheets, fuzz on the curve
of your cheeks and thighs,
your slick sweat on my skin.

And tomorrow, another hot one,
and that sweet juicy sun
will pop up again, staining
the horizon red, orange, saffron.

After the Operation, I Find I Like Sleeping Alone,

so I can keep the light on, read into the small hours,
watch the news at eleven, then drift off, not jerked
awake by your breathing, its mutter and rasp,
the percussive puffs, snorts and snores. But one night,

memory takes me around the corner, and there we are,
leaning against a stone bridge on the Île de la Cité,
tonguing cornets of *chocolat noir* from Berthillon,
the sun pouring out of the clouds like the notes
of the saxophone from the street musician on the curb—

And I am back, under the quilt, cotton in my ears,
curled tight, belly to spine, the rain playing jazz
on the roof at midnight, something small and steady
and mundane, O this daily life.

Anniversary Song
—for Richard, on our thirtieth

It's evening in the garden now
and shadows are starting to fall
on the pink coneflowers
and Russian sage, whose blue
green wands wave
in the hot wind, this late
July twilight. Fireflies rise, spiral
up from the lawn, like the tiny
light from the pointer our guide
at Font-de-Gaume used to show us
that the walls of the dark cave were alive
with bison, reindeer, horses,
the contours and bumps of the rocks
part of the painting, casting a third
dimension, the flicker of her flashlight
mimicking torches made of rush,
and suddenly a whole herd
gallops across the plains. And then,
in the last room, she traces a deer,
the parabola of his antlers arcing
above, his mate kneeling before him.
His mouth parts, his tongue reaches
down to lick her face, and across
thirty thousand years, your hand in mine,
we feel the stroke of tenderness
in the dark.

THE MOTHER SUITE

1. November
"The light of autumn: you will not be spared."
  —Louise Glück

The burning bush has given up, slipped out
of its scarlet dress, stripped down
to twig and limb, bare bones,
the architecture of itself. This is the heart
of autumn, after the fire's gone out. This is
the year's dark dying, when my mother began
to slip from sight, as imperceptibly as the moon
shifts phases; each day, a little less light. Frost's
taken all the flowers; the landscape, colorless,
shades of ash and beige, husks and seed
pods, what remains.

2. Lemon

The pebbly map of its thin skin,
the pith, the thick walls,
the tough little seeds.
It needs to be married
to sugar, white beach sands.

My mother and I are pretending
we're at the shore, sitting
on the patio of her nursing home.
A yellow raft sails off
on a sea of cold iced tea—

The citrus light of summer

washes over the moonbeam
coreopsis, the lemon lilies,
sundrops, button-headed daisies—
My mother is saying goodbye

in many little ways.
She has held her first great-
grandson; his skin's tender as a peach,
while her hands, gnarled by arthritis,
are trees left unpruned in an orchard gone wild.

O holy church of the lemon, chapel of wedges,
acidic juice, the slick shine— How the oil
clings to your skin, lingers on your fingers,
blesses the flesh of fish swimming in the plate,
kisses the filling of pie on the shelf,
remembers life is bitter,
remembers life is sweet.

3. One Word

When I told my friend from college that my son
was autistic, she said, "Why, that's wonderful. Does
he paint or draw?" And my mother, at eighty-nine,
still tries to hold on, keep the thin thread
of cognition wound around her finger,
but can't find her words: "You know what I mean,"
she tells me. "It's that thing that goes with the wash."
I play along, use Twenty Questions: "Large or small
box? Solid or liquid?" until I find out she's talking
about dryer sheets. Then there's that game
that used to appear in the Sunday papers,
where you changed one letter at a time
to create a new word at the end. So *dime*

becomes *dome* becomes *tome* becomes *tomb.*
So the afternoon leaks its light out, a letter at a time.
*Seat*ed at the round table, I *eat* toast with my mother,
make *tea.* Such a slight subtraction, for *love*
to turn to *lose.*

4. Breath

I'm thinking of it now as these clouds race by,
dolphins outlined in white, the reverse
of a child's drawing. I draw in a breath,
think of my mother's life, thinning itself down
to spindrift and salt spray. Each day, a struggle
to fill up her lungs. I'm tired of the doctors
and their weather of lies. The sky is full
now, a whole pod of porpoises, and the white
light behind them can no longer be seen.
She lingers over dinner, slow to finish her soup,
broth with tiny rafts of celery and onions, little
carrot suns. What small coins should I place
in her purse to pay the ferryman? How many breaths
do we get in this life? How many puffs of wind
to push a schooner across the sea?

5. Cold Easter

Not even early, but the weather's all turned around;
this March's colder than last December. Every day
a sputter of snow that turns the air white, but the grass
burns its green fire, and nothing sticks. "Nothing lasts,"
my mother says, fading from my eyes, and none of the fancy
tricks in the doctor's bag can make her stay. The crocuses
have already done their only trick, bursting from the hard

ground, sending up their purple flares, but the daffodils
flourish in the cold wind, small brass sections blaring
around every shrub and bush. Snow clouds roll in
from the north, erasing the sky's baby blue. Tomorrow,
Easter Sunday, I will pack a wicker basket with rare lamb,
white beans scented with rosemary, red wine, bring it
to her Country Meadows home, the last stop
before Resurrection Cemetery, across the street.
I will bring a *tarte au citron*, which I made today, grating
lemon rind, squeezing out juice, cooking it in a bain-marie
over a low flame, whisking in eggs and sugar, then unsalted
butter, pale lump by pale lump. I will bring her the sun
in a crinkled crust. Each of us will have a wedge,
bitter and sweet at the same time, that melts on the tongue,
snow on the lawn.

The Winter Sea

The ocean's gray today, like someone's dingy laundry,
the flop and slosh of sudsy waves agitate on the sand,
and the sky's the inside of an ashtray at some salty dive.
I don't care. When I took my morning walk, the blonde
grasses bowed low in the wind but did not break, and I found
a small flash of happiness in the margins, where a scrabble
of bayberry, goldenrod, pearly everlasting and milkweed
clumped together, their dried leaves and seedpods still
hanging on, no matter how hard the wind tried to knock
them down. Reduced and diminished, they remained
themselves, in spite of the elements. The way we
keep on walking each morning, as we throw off
the covers of the night and stride out on the boardwalk,
arms swinging. Yesterday at sunset, the sun's last
razzle turned the water to jewels I wanted to scoop up
and wear at my wrists and neck. Earlier, the sea
had been true blue, the color I imagine blood
might be, as it runs in my veins with the tide
of the heart. Anchor me to this world, God of spindrift,
God of spume and salt spray, God of sand. Too often,
I have let myself listen to the other voices, the ones
like Iceland gulls that shout *can't can't can't*. Right now,
fishing trawlers hang on the edge of the horizon, straight
as a clothesline, the edge you might fall over. But which,
the closer you approach, whether by sailboat, dinghy, or skiff,
is never reachable. Always, there is more.

three

*"It is the artist's duty to create a world that is more beautiful, simpler,
and more consoling than the one we live in."*
—Vincent Van Gogh (in a letter to his brother Theo)

We Are Living in Magritte Weather;

above our heads, in "The Battle of the Argonne,"
floats a luminous cloud and a granite stone,
history's opposing forces, dividing night
from day. You can't see us in the painting;
everything human's reduced in scale, the kind
of tiny town an electric train runs through.
But we're there, in the shadows, beside the small
barn, still doing our work, tending our gardens,
while generals mass their armies, and politicians plot
their next moves. Beneath our feet, more stones,
dreaming their flinty dreams. They neither yearn
for more nor envy their neighbors. They roll where
gravity takes them, gather moss and starlight.
They remember glaciers, and they praise the sun.
If you lie on the ground in the moonlight,
they will whisper what you need to save your life.

Late Turners

Under the weight of a thickly painted moon,
the keelmen heave their load of coal in the viscous
light, bringing it to Newcastle. On the right hand,
torches and small fires illuminate their toil, pierce
the haze from factories on the shore. The sky's
an argent smear. "Cobalt was good enough for him,"
one critic sniffed, not the fancier and more expensive
ultramarine. Every age has its critics, *n'est-ce pas?*
They carp and snivel around the edges, fail to see the forest
for the brushstrokes, the celestial city in the centrifugal clouds.
Later, Turner painted "Peace—Burial at Sea," which someone
snipped could read just as well upside down. He was mourning
Scottish painter David Wilkie, and said about the black sails,
"I only wish I had any color to make them blacker." The dark
boat floats on the oily sea, its single sail, a dagger in the chest.
He kept on painting, attacking the surface with his palette knife,
the swirls getting wilder, the heart's vortex, dissolving the distinction
between water and air, the imprecise measure of fog, smoke, sky.

For Judy, Whose Husband Is Undergoing Surgery
—*after Monet's "Poppy Field, Argenteuil"*

Nothing much is going on in this painting: high summer,
rolling clouds, deep blue sky. The tall poplars
fill the left hand side of the canvas; the Seine
slithers, a silvery S, barely visible through the leaves.
Someone is standing in the field, knee deep in poppies.
It could be you, before the diagnosis, when your life
seemed to spread out like a meadow of wildflowers.
The detail here is lost in the brush strokes, dots and dashes
of red and yellow, green and blue, small exclamations
of color, the sky pressing down from above. Now
you are trying to decipher the doctor's calligraphy,
the impenetrable code of sonogram and MRI, the odds
of choosing this treatment or that. The poppies flare
like matches struck in the dark, or something that should not
be there, on the monitor screen. If you were to bend
and pick them, they would wilt in your hand, the hot
orange petals falling to the ground. All you can do is raise
your face to the light, which shimmers, elusive, changes
but stays the same, a zen riddle. It's the only thing
you can hold onto, and it slips like water through your hands.

Frida Kahlo Speaks:

"Fidelity is a bourgeois virtue."
  —Diego Rivera

There are two Fridas, the one you want,
and the one you don't want. You might
have thought I wore this white dress
for you, Diego, piled this hibiscus in my hair,
threaded azul chunks of sky around my throat.
But I did it for myself. *I paint myself.* Look
at me. I wear a necklace of thorns;
a hummingbird hangs between my breasts.
My heart is a bloody shrine trapped
in a corset of pain. But I will rise,
a Bird of Paradise. I will enter your body
like a jolt of caffeine. *At last I have learned
that life is this way, and the rest is window-
dressing.* I will carve *Viva la Vida*
on this watermelon, like a tombstone. *I hope
the ending is joyful, and I hope I never return.*

Nice
—after "La Promenade des Anglais à Nice"
    —Raoul Dufy

The row of palm trees curved along the Baie des Anges
like a strand of beads on the long white neck
of a beautiful woman, and the blue Mediterranean
filled the windows of our small hotel. At night,
the waves rattled the stones like someone washing
chain mail, or a woman searching

            for something she'd lost.
Blue, blue, everywhere blue—Maritime Alpes
off in the distance, paint on this table, trim
on the walls. At the market in the *vielle ville*,
blue shellfish, crabs and mussels displayed
like needlepoint, and sea holly and lavender
in buckets in the flower stalls.

            We had never been
so far from home, without our daughters
and damaged son. Blue, blue, missing
their voices. But not-blue, this new freedom,
like slipping into a dress of silk sky, believing
I could speak another language, wear perfume
behind my ears, spend the days wandering
museums, streets with flower boxes
on every window, cobblestoned alleys,

            then nights with you in restaurants
with gilt-backed chairs, damask napkins, ruby wines.
The world of travel had licked its multicolored stamps,
pasted them all over my skin.

"The Young Girls, the Yellow Dress, and the Scottish Dress"
—Henri Matisse

I am the young woman in the butter
yellow dress; my plump arm resting
on the checked couch, same color, the one
the sun might take if it decided to become
fabric, lose its heat, come down from the sky.
My hair is pulled back from my forehead,
combed high; I look like I am ready
to dance the tarantella in a dusty square
in Naples, where half my grandparents
came from. And I am also the woman
behind her in the Scottish dress, a primary
plaid, hair the color of shortbread, eyes the color
of tea, the other half of my DNA. Behind us,
there's a wall of solid red, the way I imagine
the walls of the heart must be, that thick muscle
that keeps on beating in spite of everything,
like a faithful watch, that keeps the rivers
of the arteries flowing, bears their steady
freight. And then there's memory,
that other river, the one that meanders,
slips underground, reappears in a meadow
where you least expect it. It's a far country,
the past, and we need a passport to enter
its provinces, red oxblood with gold letters,
stamped with a blue circled visa, again
and again and again.

"The Open Window"
—Henri Matisse

I walk into this room like it's an open air market:
shutters, slabs of salmon baking on their terra cotta
bricks; window panes, peach and melon; trellis,
slashes of mustard and olive. Out of the frame,
boats sway on a candy sea, the marshmallow
sky sticky behind it, the horizon stained
with juice. In the pots in the foreground,
peppers sizzle and burn. Step back into the room,
love, and close the shutters; the walls are really
cool and white. Come out of the heat of the day,
the dazzling sun. There are just the two of us here,
no telephones, watches, deadlines, and we can make
the afternoon stretch behind the closed slats,
on the smooth ironed sheets. The outside world
clatters away, traffic and klaxons, the blaring of horns.
The sun seethes behind the shutters, edible, volatile.

"The Shell"
—oil pastel by Odilon Redon

I was walking on the beach, looking for something,
but I didn't know what, a piece of sand dollar
or broken whelk, a bit of glass, something
that would remind me of this day,
with the Gulf shimmering like a skillet of sapphires,
fat puffy clouds inflated by the wind. The palm trees
were playing their usual refrain, clatter and rasp,
clatter and rasp, and evening was coming down,
the undersides of the cumulus turning pink
as a tropical drink. And then, in the turquoise surf,
although surf's too big a word for these small waves,
this gentle lapping in the shallows, I saw it,
rolling and tumbling in the lacy froth,
an unbroken conch shell, its pale pink lip
an echo of the sky that deepens, pinkens
by the minute, as the planet does its
nightly pirouette. If I pick it up and hold it
to my ear, with its own swoops and whorls,
I might hear the cool voice of God. Or I might
hear my mother calling, "It's time to come in
now, hush, hush."

At the Renoir Landscape Exhibit
—*Philadelphia Art Museum*

We sat at the café like Renoir's models, letting the sun daub us
with licks of light, flicks of a sable brush. The way your fingertips
had grazed my cheek that night, painted it peach and cream.
Now we are looking at a painting of dahlias, a diagonal tumble
of red, gold, white, but I am back in that garden in St. Germain-
en-Laye, only now it's twilight that's brushing our arms violet
and mauve. We're having dinner, and this is a *luxe* group,
women in understated black sheaths, pearls on slender necks,
expensive shawls flung carelessly over bare white arms.
We're in a different life, an expense account, with a couple
from headquarters for whom this is a matter of course.
She checks her cell phone, taps her fingernails impatiently
between courses. Her husband urges me to try the *foie gras*,
let it melt on crisp toast, sip the topaz notes of the sweet aperitif
that cuts through the richness, enhances the tone. The garden
in twilight: enormous globe thistles, heavy mauve cabbage roses,
the scents of exquisite perfumes. . . . And later, in our small
hotel, you with your deft little brush strokes on the linen
of my skin. . . . The rhythm, as we rowed our way towards shore,
like the girls in the skiff in this painting in their bright summer
dresses and jaunty hats. You dip your oar in the shimmering
water again and again, until the canvas is streaked with brilliant
slashes of red/yellow/orange, blue/dark blue/green, a wave
collapsing on the rocky shore, then dissolving into itself
in foam, vapor, light.

THREE BY HOPPER

1. "Gas"

I like the loneliness of old gas stations,
Pegasus, a faded red, about to fly off
into the sky, which stretches above the dark
pines, the rural road running by, a river,
all curves and meanders. The white paint's
flaked off the wooden shingles,
and the *Drink Coca-Cola!* sign is stained
with rust, but the light in the window
casts a yellow glow on the cement.

I think my parents are about to cruise up
in their Buick, a big gray boat of a car,
the one that was up on blocks during the war,
and they have no idea what darkness lies
ahead. She's happy, leaning back
on the plush seat, the night air riffling
her page boy; he leans his arm out the window,
the ash of his cigarette eddying to the ground.

The lone attendant fills their tank, checks the oil,
wipes both windshields until they gleam, then returns
to his metal chair, his solitary vigil, keeper
of the lighthouse, pilot of the night.

2. "Chop Suey"

We were sitting in that little Chinese restaurant
you used to like, the distance between us,
like the cold Formica table, vast as a shelf

of ice. It was so quiet, you could hear each tick
of the clock as the minute hand hit
another notch. I saw you checking your watch
when you thought I wasn't looking, your glance
glazing off to the side. You were ready to leave
as soon as we arrived. Our eyes don't meet, ocean
liners in separate shipping lanes. In the middle
of the table, the tea in the pot continued its slow steep,
though we both knew how bitter it will taste
when the waiter finally brings the tiny porcelain cups.

3. Hopper's Women
— *"High Noon"*

are always alone, even if someone
else is in the room, even if they're leaning
at the counter of an all-night diner. This woman
is standing in the open mouth of her doorway
as if it were the prow of an ocean liner,
ready to embark on a long voyage. Her dress
and lips part in anticipation. The sun pounds
down, a relentless spotlight, but she is unblinking
in its glare, stares off in the middle distance.
Triangular shadows slice the air; rough waters
ahead. The curtain of the sky rises. Everything
is about to begin.

four

"All I ever wanted was more."
—anonymous six word memoir

Gray Foxes

It was the summer the gray foxes came out
of the deep woods to stand on our suburban lawn,
screaming at the dying cat, claiming the night for their own.
Two nights later, he faded away, became dust and stone.

After surgery, my mother hallucinated that she was alone
in the hospital, the last person on earth. She
picked up the phone, but there was no one to call.
Night after night, she had the same dream,
the only one alive in a deserted city.

And then the black day came when the old dog left us;
his breath, ragged, foam bubbling from his muzzle.
He laid his head down in the dew-drenched grass,
a sweet September morning, and never got up again.

Maybe the foxes were real; maybe they were only a dream.
The days rush by, swallows in the wind with their green backs
and white throats; they disappear in the shadows
when twilight overtakes them.

My Life as a Song Sparrow

My life is a song sparrow, chip chip chipping
on the hard white ground, hoping to find seeds,
yellow millet or black sunflower. It flits
from old apple tree to hedgerow, saying
my name. It's ordinary as this day,
beige, brown, and white, not flashy cardinal red,
not brassy jaybird blue. You'd hardly notice it
at the feeder, jostled out by all those bigger
birds, plain as the hills behind us, stippled
with trees. It's both more and less than I was
hoping for as I think about the cold mountain,
the long journey home. The sparrow looks
in the still water as it sits on the lip of the bird
bath, sees the wind-drawn ripples. It doesn't look
for more than food and shelter, a nest of straw,
a bough to keep off snow. Someone to share
a branch with, downy feathers on a night
of frozen zeroes. What more can a person
hope for, in this world of a thousand sorrows,
than a life that was made for song, than a body
sometimes able to take wing?

Family Album

The dead calla lily rose
like a cobra from the hood of its pot.
I wanted to break off the dried
stalk, but I was at my grandmother's;
it wasn't my place. In her dining
room, the Chianti-colored walls bloomed
with photographs: birthdays, weddings,
first communions, with crosses made of dried
palms tucked behind each frame, and Jordan
almonds clustered in nylon netting on the credenza.
We were in our Sunday best, itchy and starched.
Nona brought in the ravioli, the sausage,
the chicken, the bowls of blood-red *ragù*.

No one in this snapshot is still living, swallowed
by the darkness charmed like a snake from its basket
of coils. On this November afternoon, with a cold front
coming in, the sun, a pale grapefruit in an orchard of clouds,
I close this black album, with all of its stories, including
the ones that haven't been written, including the ones
that nobody's told.

Ghazal: One Summer

It was nineteen sixty-eight, The Summer of Love;
patchouli and marijuana hung in the air, a murmur of love.

We came to San Francisco in a Volkswagen Bug,
rust-red, my heart, back-beat drummer of love.

I wore a peasant dress, my hair hung down my back;
you'd let yours grow into an Afro, sideburns, latecomer to love.

I thought "forever" meant it, that we were only tourists
at the Be-In, didn't see your eyes rove. A bummer, this love.

We became a statistic, cliché, another marriage gone bad.
I raised our daughter; you had a number of lovers.

My life, a rainbow fish hauled up on hooks and barbs, dulled,
dimmed. Cast-off old tie-dye, could I have been dumber, in love?

Firstborn

—2-2-70

The sun came up, as it always does,
the next morning, its pale yolk
bleeding into the white room.
I remember how cold I was,
and how young, so thin,
my wedding ring rattled
on my finger. How the tea
the nurse brought
broke in waves on the rim
of the cup, spilled over
in the saucer; how nothing
could contain my tears.
Three days later, I left
in a wheelchair,
with nothing in my arms.
The center of this ring
is a zero. The horizon,
where the sun broke through,
is no longer a straight line,
but a circle. It all comes back
to you.

Glitter

The last line comes from a lecture by art historian Helen Kwiatkowski.

The monk who discovered champagne said
Come quickly, brothers, I am tasting stars,
but I think I'm sipping glitter tonight,
my blood turning fizzy, words sharp and witty,
a party going on in my mouth—

Is this what God was thinking when she riddled
the night sky, spangled the black
firmament, glammed up the dark reaches
of infinity?

I think of myself at thirty, my turn for playgroup,
six small children at the kitchen table, sheets of navy
and black construction paper, making snow scenes
with daubs of white glue and glitter sprinkled
from waxed paper cones. There was paste
in their hair, bits of paper stuck to clothes,
but each chubby cheek was dusted
in gold, and silver glinted on stubby hands—

Last month, I'd been away in the South, returned
to the dullness of January, Christmas tree down,
ornaments put away, the landscape colorless,
too cold even for birds— As the plane
made its long descent, I saw the city
spread out below, the sparkle of streetlights,
the grid of lit windows, the strung beads
of headlights and brakes, high beams piercing
the darkness in splinters of light.
Everything looks better with glitter on it.

Yes

"Yes was the best answer to every question."
     —*Frank McCourt, <u>Teacher Man</u>*

So I said yes to everything, yes to the green hills
rolling out ahead, yes to the hayfield tied up in rolls,
yes to the clouds blooming like peonies in the sky's
blue meadow, the long tongue of the road lolling
out before me, yes to the life of travel, yes to the other
life at home, yes to the daisies freckling the ditch,
to the sun pouring down on everything
like Vermeer's milkmaid and her endless
jug of milk, yes to the winds that pulled the clouds
apart like taffy, then turned them into a classroom
of waving hands punched into fists: *yes yes yes.*

Ash Wednesday,

butt-end of winter, and my brother-in-law's cancer
has returned from whatever cave it was lurking in.
Flocks of grackles have come back, jabbing
their cross stitches on the sky's pale muslin.
Multiplicands of darkness, they beat their wings
like swimmers, parting the air which closes
behind them, seamlessly. They flow in a current,
tree to tree, crossing the road. Clatter and clack,
they pass along those old stories of rebirth and renewal,
impossible rumors of green grass, blue skies, sweet air.
How can we remember we are dust, when that red river
and its blue tributaries runs like a stream over stones?
Ashes kiss my forehead. Candles mark the dark.
Greedy beaks, beady yellow eyes.

Strewn

It'd been a long winter, rags of snow hanging on; then, at the end
of April, an icy nor'easter, powerful as a hurricane. But now
I've landed on the coast of Maine, visiting a friend who lives
two blocks from the ocean, and I can't believe my luck,
out this mild morning, race-walking along the strand.
Every dog within fifty miles is off-leash, running
for the sheer dopey joy of it. No one's in the water,
but walkers and shellers leave their tracks on the hardpack.
The flat sand shines as if varnished in a painting. Underfoot,
strewn, are broken bits and pieces, deep indigo mussels, whorls
of whelk, chips of purple and white wampum, hinges of quahog,
fragments of sand dollars. Nothing whole, everything
broken, washed up here, stranded. The light pours down, a rinse
of lemon on a cold plate. All of us, broken, some way
or other. All of us dazzling in the brilliant slanting light.

Holsteins

I'm walking down a gravel road,
past cows in the green fields,

whose teeth making a kind of music
slowly chewing their way across the meadow.

The black one with the white face reminds me
of a girl from school, the way she rounded

her shoulders trying to hide her bulk
as she shoveled in lunch, the way she looked

middle-aged at fourteen, chins gleaming
as if she'd been grazing on buttercups,

her cardigans, flowered dresses, sensible shoes.
But I saw her at the last reunion, and she'd lost

the weight, stepped out of that old life
and into another. Anything can happen.

A cow can grow wings, become an American
Redstart, flit black-and-white from tree

to tree. A woman can lean on a rusty fence
and get tired of wishing things would change.

But I don't want to change a thing. I want
to keep walking this stony path, listening

to dried leaves in the beech tree,
insects playing their strings in the grass.

I want the sun to run down my face like honey.
I want the wind to kiss me. I want all this to last.

Acknowledgments

The Anglican Theological Review: "Yes"

Apalachee Review: "Excuses, Excuses"

Ars Medica: "The Sun Lays Down its Light"

Borderlands: The Texas Poetry Review: "Chop Suey"

Calyx: "Firstborn"

Christianity and Literature: "Cold Easter," "Lemon"

Concho River Review: "Peaches"

The Innisfree Poetry Journal: "November," "At the Renoir Landscape Exhibit," "Family Album"

Green Mountains Review: "Late Turners," "Winter Sea"

Louisiana Literature: "We Are Living in Magritte Weather;"

The MacGuffin: "The Open Window," "Ode to Chocolate," "Hopper's Women," "The Young Girls, the Yellow Dress and the Scottish Dress"

Natural Bridge: "Frida Kahlo Speaks:"

Persimmon Tree: "Surfer Girl"

Perspectives: "Ode to Olive Oil," "My Life as a Song Sparrow"

The Pittsburgh Post-Gazette: "Finches, Little Pats of Butter on the Wing,"

Poetry International: "Anniversary Song," "Nice"

River City: "What You Want"

Rock & Sling: "Our Lady of Rocamadour," "Sanctus"

Rosebud: "For Judy, Whose Husband Is Undergoing Surgery," "Gas"

Superstition Review: "Ghazal: One Summer," "Demeter"

Tampa Review: "Gray Foxes"

Tattoo Highway: "After the Operation, I Find I Like Sleeping Alone,"

Tiferet: "Breath"

The Valparaiso Poetry Review: "One Word"

Windhover: "Ash Wednesday," "Glitter," "How the Trees on Summer Nights Turn into a Dark River," "Salt," "Demeter"

The Writer: "Salt"

"Geology" Copyright © 2005 by the *Christian Century* and reprinted by permission. "Strewn" Copyright © 2009 by the *Christian Century* and reprinted by permission. "Narrative" Copyright © 2006 by *Christian Century* and reprinted by permission.

"What You Want" appeared in the *2007 Women Artists Date Book* (Syracuse Cultural Workers Press).

"Demeter" appeared in the *Pen and Brush Anthology.*

"Ode to Chocolate" appeared in *No Direct Route Home* (Woodrow Hall Editions) and *Breathe: 101 Contemporary Odes* (C&R Press).

"Snapshot" appeared in *They Wrote Us a Poem IX* (HAND, Duke University).

"Demeter" won the 2007 Pen and Brush Poetry Contest; "Gas" won the 2006 *Rosebud* Ekphrastic Poetry Contest.

Many thanks to the Virginia Center for the Creative Arts for the gift of space and silence, to my friends in writing: Diane Lockward, Rachel Dacus, Ken Fifer, Joan Mazza, Angela O'Donnell, Alan and Alice Berecka, Barbara Reisner, Kathy Moser, and Geri Rosenzweig, who looked at many of the poems in this manuscript; Dick Allen, for his excellent advice; my husband, Dick; and my children, Stacey, Rebecca, David; and my grandson, Daniel.